Threads books

Beans
Bread (also in paperback)
Bricks
Clay
Cotton
Eggs
Fruit
Glass
Milk (also in paperback)
Paper (also in paperback)
Plastics (also in paperback)
Rice
Rocks
Salt
Silk
Spices
Tea
Water (also in paperback)
Wood (also in paperback)
Wool

A CIP catalogue record for this book is available from the British Library.

ISBN 0–7136–2930–4

First published by A & C Black (Publishers) Ltd
35 Bedford Row, London WC1R 4JH

©1987 A & C Black (Publishers) Ltd
Reprinted 1989, 1991

Acknowledgements
Illustrations by Caroline Ewen
Photographs by Ed Barber, except p 6 Barrie Watts, p 21 The Federation of Bakers, p 24 (top) Sally Fear.

The author and publisher would like to thank the Flour Advisory Bureau for their advice, and the staff and pupils of Bonner Primary School without whose help and cooperation this book would not have been possible.

Filmset by August Filmsetting, Haydock, St Helens
Printed in Belgium by Proost International Book Production

Bread

Judith Baskerville

Photographs by Ed Barber

Contents

A & C Black · London

What goes into bread?

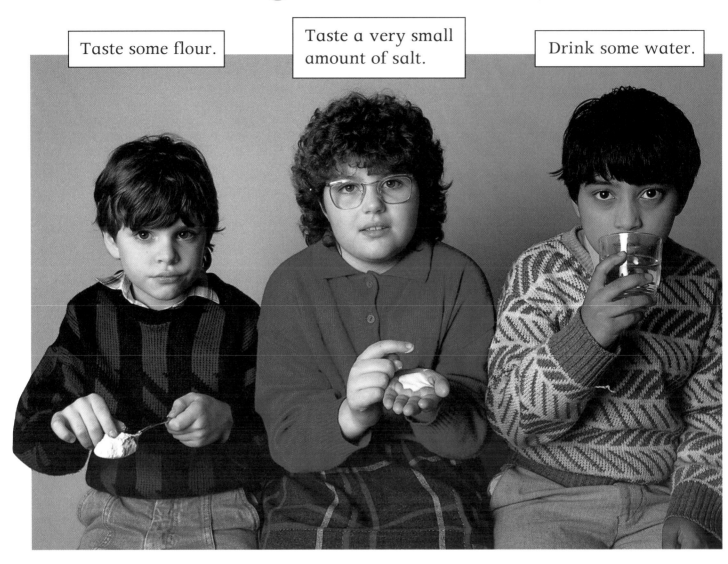

Taste some flour.

Taste a very small amount of salt.

Drink some water.

How would you describe the tastes?
Water is a good drink, but it doesn't have much flavour. The flour and the salt are not very nice at all.

Try mixing them together and maybe this will improve the taste? What do you think?

It's hard to believe that
this mixture will make
something you probably eat
every day – bread.

Bread that is good for you.
Bread in all kinds of shapes,
sizes, and colours.
Bread with different textures
and tastes.
Bread that is eaten almost
all over the world.

Flour

Have a look at some different kinds of bread. Taste some with your eyes closed. Can you taste any differences?

Now take a closer look. What colour is the bread? Does it have any 'bits' in it? If it does, try to remove them. What do you think they are?

Remember the mixture of flour, salt, and water which you made? It's the flour which gives bread its colour and texture.

The flour comes from cereal plants, like these. It's made by grinding, or crushing, the seeds of the plants.

Oats

Rye

Barley

Millet

Maize

Wheat

Seeds (sometimes called grains).

Have you ever noticed the names of these plants on packets of breakfast cereal?

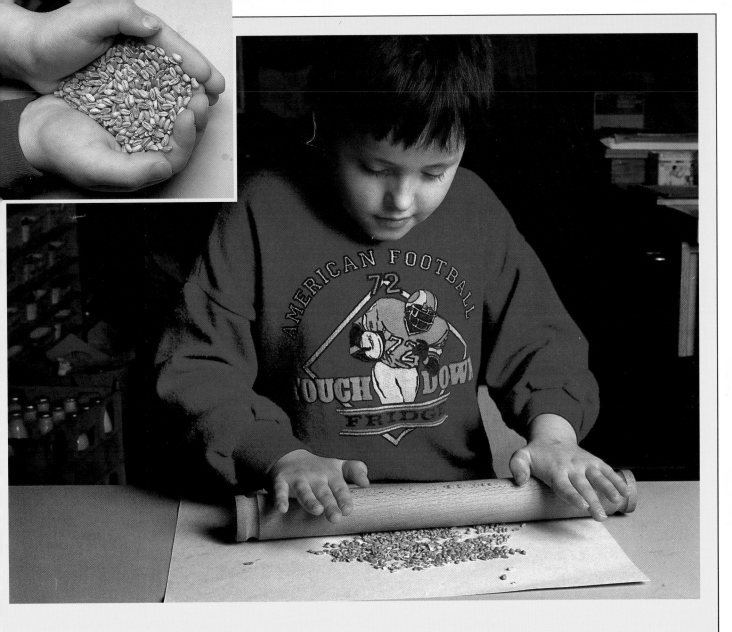

You could try grinding your own flour from
cereal plants. You will need some cereal grain
(you can buy wheat grain from health food
shops) and a tool for grinding. Try using two
stones, or a rolling pin. You'll find that it's very
hard work. That's why, nowadays, most flour
is made by machine and the grains are ground
between huge steel rollers.

Almost all the different kinds of flour which you see in the shops are made from wheat grains, like these.

Try cutting a grain of wheat down the middle. If you look at it through a magnifying glass, you'll see that it has three main parts.

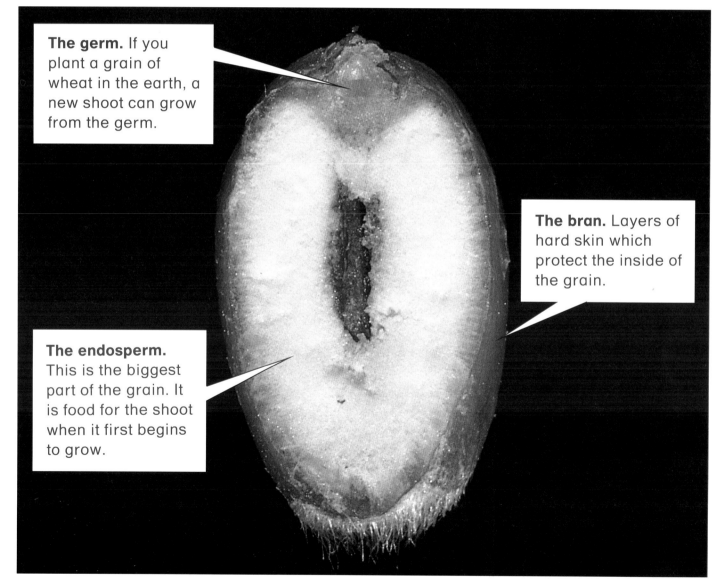

The germ. If you plant a grain of wheat in the earth, a new shoot can grow from the germ.

The bran. Layers of hard skin which protect the inside of the grain.

The endosperm. This is the biggest part of the grain. It is food for the shoot when it first begins to grow.

These flours are all made from different parts
of the wheat grain.

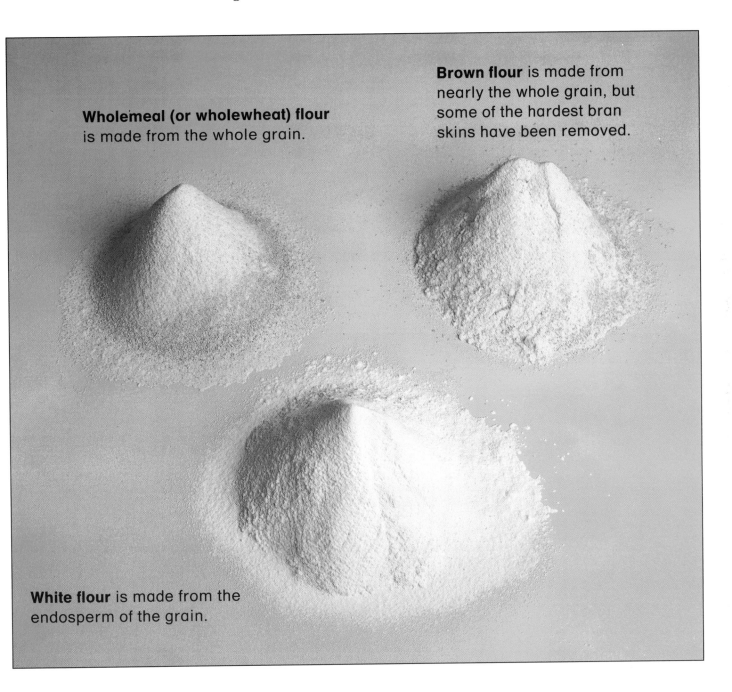

Wholemeal (or wholewheat) flour
is made from the whole grain.

Brown flour is made from
nearly the whole grain, but
some of the hardest bran
skins have been removed.

White flour is made from the
endosperm of the grain.

What kinds of bread could you make from these flours?
Try to imagine the colour and texture of the bread.

What makes bread rise?

There is something which makes wheat flour special
and different from nearly all other cereal flours.
These rotis are made from wheat flour and water.
Have a close look at them.

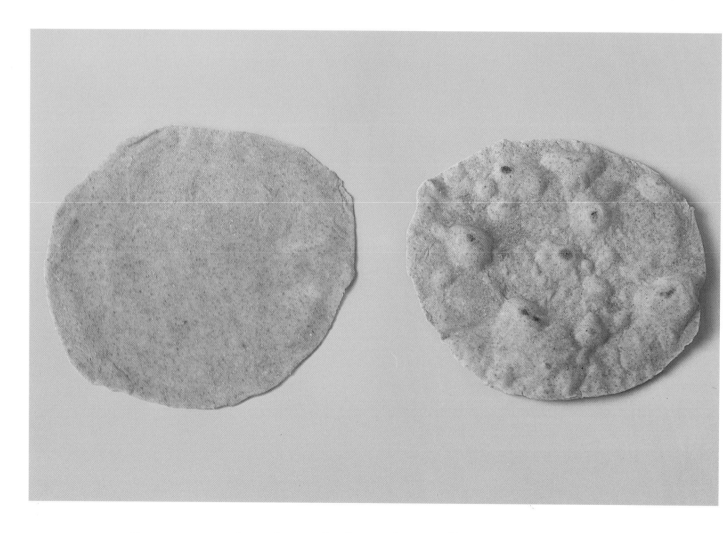

Can you see that the cooked roti has puffed up?
It has risen slightly. When wheat flour is mixed with
the right amount of water, a new substance,
called gluten, is created.

Try making gluten

You will need

Oven, set at 230°C (450°F) or Gas Mark 8.

2 tablespoons of water

50 g of flour

How to do it

1. Mix the flour and water together to make a smooth dough. Roll the dough into a ball and soak it in a bowl of cold water for half an hour. Then gently fold and squeeze the dough under a running tap.

2. After about five minutes, you will be left with just the gluten. What does it look and feel like?

3. Cook the gluten in the oven for about 20 minutes. Let it cool and then have a good look at it. How much does it weigh? Try cutting it open.

Gluten stretches, rather like chewing gum. When it is heated, it blows up like a bubble. Imagine lots of tiny bubbles being blown up inside the roti. No wonder the roti rises when it is cooked.

9

Look at all the bubbles in this slice of bread.

The gluten in wheat flour makes bread rise a little bit. But something else is often added to bread, to make it rise even more.

Can you tell which of these breads have been cooked with this extra ingredient?

Usually, a special plant, called yeast, is the extra ingredient which makes bread rise, although chemicals are sometimes used instead.

Like all plants, yeast is alive and it needs food, water, and warmth.

If you want to see how yeast works, try this.

You will need

A little warm water

2 teaspoons of sugar

2 teaspoons of fresh yeast

Mix them all together and watch what happens.

After 10 minutes, bubbles appear round the edge of the bowl – keep watching. After 40 minutes, the surface will be frothy.

The yeast is feeding on the sugar. As it feeds, it makes the bubbles of gas which you can see.

When yeast is mixed with flour and water to make bread, it feeds on part of the flour and makes bubbles of gas in the bread. This is what makes the bread rise. Try making your own bread and see what happens.

How to make bread

You will need

250 ml very warm water

½ teaspoon of salt

400 g brown flour

2 mixing bowls

15 g fresh yeast

Greased baking tray

Large polythene bag

Oven set to 230°C (450°F) Gas Mark 8

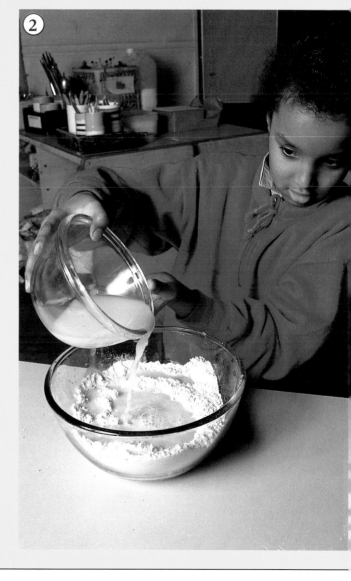

How to do it

1. Mix the flour and salt together in a bowl. In another bowl, mix the yeast with the water. Keep stirring until all the yeast has mixed in properly.

2. Make a well in the flour and pour the yeast liquid into it. Then mix them up. This makes the dough.

3. Sprinkle some flour on to a clean flat surface. Then tip the dough on to it. Fold the dough in half and press down on it. Keep folding and pressing until the dough stops being sticky. This is called kneading, and it will take at least 5 minutes.

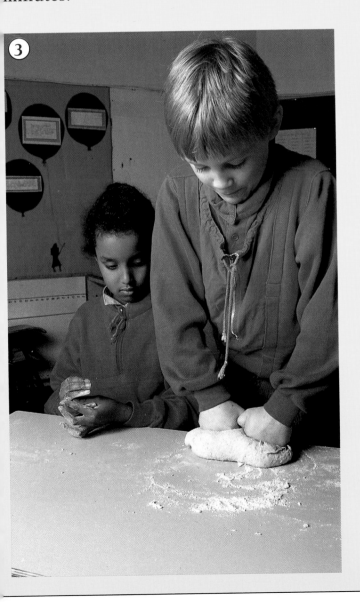

4. Cut the dough into 10 pieces and roll each piece into a ball. Put the balls of dough on to a greased baking tray and put the tray carefully into a polythene bag. Then leave the dough in a warm place to rise.

After about 50 minutes, the dough will have doubled in size. The yeast has done its work. Take the baking tray out of the polythene bag.

5. Bake the dough in the oven for 10–15 minutes. The heat will stop the yeast from working any more. The yeast helps to give baking bread its lovely smell.

Let your rolls cool. Then you can eat them.

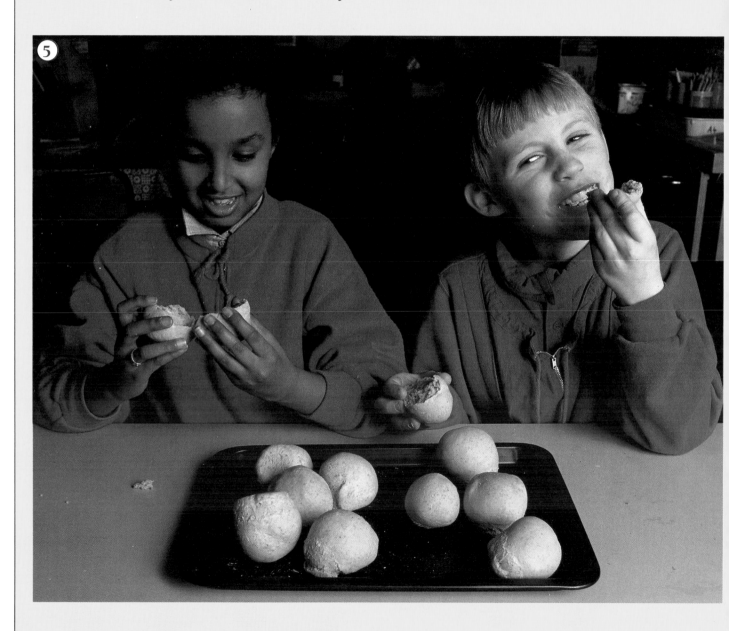

Remember tasting the flour, salt and water?
What a difference!

You can use your bread dough to make lots of different things to eat. Here are some ideas to get you started. (There are some recipes at the back of the book.)

Roll the dough flat and make pizzas.

Try adding dried fruit and nuts.

Put seeds like poppy or sesame on the top.

How the sandwich got its name

You could use your rolls, or different kinds of bread, to make sandwiches. Swap ideas with your friends. You might be able to invent a brilliant new kind of sandwich.

The sandwich got its name from a man called the Earl of Sandwich, who lived about two hundred years ago. He enjoyed playing cards so much that he never wanted to stop for meals. One day, he asked for a piece of meat to be served between two slices of bread, so he could eat while he was playing. The name sandwich has stuck ever since.

In the bakery

In your family, do you bake your own bread or buy it at a supermarket or bakery?

This supermarket has a bakery behind the shop. The bakers start work at three o'clock each morning, so that the bread will be ready when the supermarket opens.

The baker starts by mixing up the yeast, flour and water in a big machine. Then he takes out a lump of dough and cuts it into pieces.

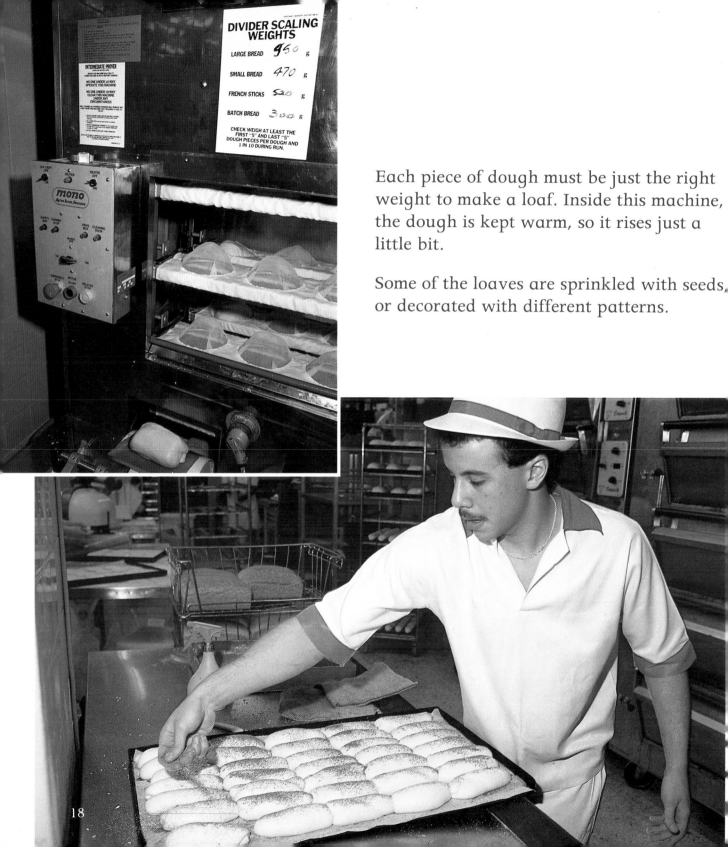

DIVIDER SCALING WEIGHTS

LARGE BREAD	960 g
SMALL BREAD	470 g
FRENCH STICKS	520 g
BATCH BREAD	300 g

CHECK WEIGH AT LEAST THE FIRST "5" AND LAST "5" DOUGH PIECES PER DOUGH AND 1 IN 10 DURING RUN.

Each piece of dough must be just the right weight to make a loaf. Inside this machine, the dough is kept warm, so it rises just a little bit.

Some of the loaves are sprinkled with seeds, or decorated with different patterns.

The loaves are put into a big steam cupboard, and the warm air and steam inside make the bread rise. Here's the bread being taken out of the steam cupboard.

Now the loaves are ready to go into the oven.

The baker keeps checking the loaves to see if they are ready.

When the bread is cooked, it is stacked on racks to cool, and then goes straight down to the shop.

Slicing and wrapping

Some of the bread you buy in the shops is made in big factories, like this one. The bread is cooked in huge ovens and goes down a conveyor belt to be sliced and wrapped. Then it is taken by lorry to different shops and supermarkets.

The companies who make and sell this bread put their own design on the wrapping. Have a look at some different types of wrapping. Can you find any facts written on them? You could design your own wrapping and make up a catchy name for your loaf.

Bread with everything

Bread goes well with so many different things.

Bread pudding

Pizza

Roti with dhal

A hamburger with a bun

Toast and marmalade

Pitta bread with kebabs

How many times have you
eaten bread this week?

23

Bread for celebrations

Bread is so important to us, that it is often made for special occasions.
Here are two different kinds of bread made for festivals.

Matzos, which Jewish people eat at their
Passover celebrations.

A harvest loaf, which Christians bake for
Harvest Festival.

What celebrations have you been to where
bread has been served? Was it an important
part of the celebration?

We eat bread so often that it seems rather
ordinary, but your next bite should give
you a lot to think about.

More things to do

1. Try making a fruit and nut loaf. To make the dough, use steps 1–3 of the recipe on pages 12–13. Put the dough in a greased polythene bag and leave to rise for about 1 hour. Then add 150 gms of chopped dates, raisins or chopped dried apricots; 50 gms of chopped walnuts; 25 gms of caster sugar; 25 gms of butter or margarine. Squeeze and work these into the dough.

Make the dough into a loaf shape and put into a large, greased loaf tin, cover and leave to rise again for about 45 minutes. Bake in a hot oven, 220°C (425°F), Gas mark 7 for about 50 minutes. Cool on a wire rack.

2. Think of some experiments to try when you are making bread. Think about the weight and volume of the bread. Talk about your ideas with your friends before you start.

3. Bread which is cooked with an extra ingredient to make it rise is called leavened bread and it is usually cooked in an oven. Flat bread is called unleavened bread and it is usually cooked on a hot surface, like a tava or heavy frying pan. Next time you go to the supermarket, see how many different kinds of leavened and unleavened bread you can find. Don't be afraid to ask the names of the ones you don't know.

4. Try cooking some flat bread. Rotis are quite easy to make. Ask an adult to help you.
You will need: 225 gms of chapatti flour (*or* 100 gms of whole-wheat flour and 100 gms of plain white flour); 190 ml of water; a bowl; a heavy non-stick frying pan; a rolling pin.
How to do it: Mix the flour and water together and knead for about 5–10 minutes. Cover the bowl of dough with a damp cloth and leave for 20 minutes. Then roll the dough into 12 balls. Flatten each ball and roll out on a floury surface to make a flat circle about 12 cm across. Heat up the frying pan and then put in a roti. Cook for one minute each side. To make the roti puff up you can put it under a hot grill for a few seconds, or press the edges gently with a tea towel.

5. Bread helps you to keep fit and healthy because it contains vitamins, minerals and roughage. Have a look at the labels on wrapped bread and try to find out more about what it contains.

Index

(Numbers in **bold** type are pages which show activities.)